This book belongs to:

........Sappire...

Teacher:

..........williams......................................

Grade:

..........3rd......................................

KIDS DREAMS MATTER Publishing, Inc.

Greensboro, NC

ISBN: 978-1-7366185-1-6

What Should I Eat Today?

by Audretta Hall and Robert Krumroy
illustrated and designed by Ugur Kose and Donna West

— Contents —

What should I eat today?

What should I eat today that will help me laugh, run and play?

Should I have milk for my bones?

Something with Vitamin D for my knees?

What should I eat today that will help me play the WHOLE day?

How about something whole grain to help my body and my brain?

$$4 \times 1 = 4$$
$$4 \times 2 = 8$$
$$4 \times 3 = 12$$

$$\left(\frac{4+4}{3}\right) xy = ab^2$$

$$1 + 1 = 2$$

Or even a snack of some fruit and nuts?

That should be simple to fix and easy for you to cut up!

What should I eat today that will increase my ability to run, jump, and play?

9

I know, something red, yellow, and GREEN - to help my body stay strong and lean.

Wow, I might even have some beans - I think that they are high in bodybuilding protein!

What should I eat today that will make me feel good, play longer, and help you more?

I am ready! Let's go to the grocery store.

There we can pick up all the things on my list and MORE.

I am looking forward to eating today all the things that will help me laugh louder, run further, and do all of my chores.

What shall I eat today?

All the things that help me do MORE!

The "Traffic Light Foods" Method

The "Traffic Light Foods" Method

Can Help You Make Healthy Food Choices!

In the Traffic Light Foods program, all foods are classified as Red, Yellow, or Green light. These lists can help you learn which foods are the healthiest!

– GREEN LIGHT FOODS –

Green Light foods = GO!

Green Light foods have high nutritional value and are low in calories, sugar, and fat. These foods are the healthiest choices for children, but many kids do not get enough of these foods every day. The best way to make sure you are getting enough Green Light foods is to eat at least one fruit and one vegetable at every meal with milk or water. Green Light foods have nutrients to give you energy and help your body grow!

All Whole Fresh Fruits

Asparagus

Beans and Lentils

Broccoli

Brussels Sprouts

Cabbage

Cauliflower

Chicken (Baked, not Fried)

Coconut Water

Coffee

Cucumbers

Eggs

English Muffin

Fish (Grilled or Baked)

Greek Yogurt

Greens (Collard, Turnip, Mustard, etc.)

Lettuce

Milk

Mushrooms

Mustards (All)

Nuts (Almonds, Pecans, Walnuts, etc.)

Okra

Oatmeal

Peanut Butter

Tomatoes

Turkey

Zucchini

– YELLOW LIGHT FOODS –

Yellow Light foods = Slow Down.

Yellow Light foods make up much of our diet. Though many contain important nutrients, some should be substituted with foods with lower calories and higher nutritional value. Be aware of how much you eat and your portion size when snacking.

Beef - Oven Roasted or Broiled (Not Fast Food Hamburger!)

Bread (Whole Grain or Wheat - not White)

Bulgur

Butter (Use Sparingly)

Corn

Cottage Cheese (Low Fat)

Deli Turkey or Chicken for Sandwiches

Granola (Low Fat)

Green Peas

Grits (With Light Butter, Not Cheese)

Mozzarella Cheese

Pasta (Whole Wheat)

Pork / Ham (Oven Roasted)

Potatoes (High in Calories - Watch Portion Size)

Salad Dressing

Sweet Potatoes (Healthier than White Potatoes)

Winter Squashes

- RED LIGHT FOODS -

Red Light foods = STOP and Think.

Red Light foods have very little, if any, nutritional value. Eating too many of these foods can cause significant weight gain. They tend to be high in calories, sugar, and harmful fats. Limit these foods.

ALL FAST FOODS (Tacos, Burgers - Limit to Once a Week)

ALL FRIED FOODS (Fish, Chicken, Chicken Nuggets, Okra, Beef)

Bacon

Biscuits (Avoid - High Cholesterol, Fat and Calories)

Bologna, Salami, Spam

Bread or Buns (White - Substitute Wheat or Wraps)

Brownies / Cookies / Cakes / Pies

Candy Bars

Cereals with High Sugar (Mostly Children's Brands)

Cheese and Cheese Spreads

Chips or Popcorn in a Bag

Coleslaw (Mayonnaise-Based)

Cupcakes

Doughnuts

Fish Sticks

Flavored Yogurt

French Fries

Fruit (in Cans with Heavy Syrup)

Fruit Juice Boxes

Grilled Cheese Sandwiches

Hot Dogs

Ice Cream

Lard

Mac and Cheese

Margarine (Substitute Olive Oil)

Mayonnaise (Regular)

Pancakes and Syrup

Pasta (Limit Regular Pasta to Once a Week)

Pastries & Breakfast Tarts

Pizza (Limit to Once a Week)

Potato Salad

Soda

Sports Drinks

Sweet Iced Tea

Wow – Look at All of Your Food Choices!

X All of the Red Light Foods

O Circle All of the Yellow Light Foods

✓ All of the Green Light Foods

26

milk

Water

Wheat Bread

Baked Chicken

Bulgur

Mozzarella Cheese

Wild Rice

Fried Chicken Nuggets

27

Draw Your Own Healthy Breakfast:

Be sure to include Fruits, Grains, Protein Foods, and Dairy!

Draw Your Own Healthy Lunch:

Be sure to include Fruits, Vegetables, Grains, Protein Foods, and Dairy!

Draw Your Own Healthy Dinner:

Be sure to include Fruits, Vegetables, Grains, Protein Foods, and Dairy!

Cooking With Kids:

Younger cooks require vigilant supervision. You will need to perform tasks, such as cutting and peeling, for them. You might wish to demonstrate the correct way to hold and use dangerous kitchen equipment.

Have a fire safety conversation. It's important to stress fire safety basics.

To My Parent:

The following pages contain recipes that can enhance our family's health, my health and even my ability to perform well in school. Just a few small dietary changes, such as staying away from RED LIGHT foods and adding more GREEN LIGHT foods can make a big difference. Maybe we can start considering some changes by making a surprise dinner together from the recipes on the following pages.

Did you know that eating just 250 extra calories in a day (a single soda and a candy bar) will add 12 pounds of weight in one year? Daily calories matter.

Here are some facts that we should pay extra attention to:

1 Soda - 150 calories

1 Glass of Sweet Iced Tea - 100 calories

2 Oreo Cookies - 140 calories

1 Candy Bar - 180 calories

French Fries (Regular Order) - 260 calories
(A Large Order - 560 calories)

1 Serving of Potato Chips - 150 calories

1 Muffin - 500 calories

1 Pack of Kid's Dessert Snacks - 300 calories

1 Cupcake - 400 calories

Student Assignment:

Pick one of the following recipes to prepare with a parent, or a household adult. Write a paragraph on what you enjoyed about the experience and the recipe you selected.

_____

_____

_____

_____

_____

Quick and Healthy Lemon Chicken Breasts
SERVES: 4 | CALORIES: 400

Ingredients

- 4 chicken breasts (remove skin)
- 2 tablespoons olive oil
- 6 tablespoons lemon juice
- 1 tablespoon Italian spices, oregano, or herbes de Provence
- salt and pepper

Directions

Pour the oil, lemon juice and herbs into a bowl or large 1 gallon freezer bag.

Place the chicken breasts in the dish or bag and cover the chicken breasts with the mixture. Let them marinate for 5 or 10 minutes.

Heat a non-stick frying pan over medium heat. Add the chicken and marinade; cook for 10 - 15 minutes, until cooked through.

Salt and pepper to taste. Enjoy!

Easy, Delicious, Healthy Meatloaf
SERVES: 4-5 | CALORIES: 400

Ingredients

- 1½ pounds extra lean ground beef (1 pound for 3 people)
- 1 large onion (diced into small pieces)
- 1 green bell pepper (diced into small pieces)
- 1 cup carrots – (1 medium carrot, shredded)
- 3 garlic cloves (chopped)
- 1 egg
- salt and pepper to taste
- 1 cup dried bread crumbs
- 1 cup milk
- sauce: mix ½ cup ketchup, 3 tablespoons mustard, 1 tablespoon brown sugar
- olive oil

Directions

Use a 9 x 5 inch loaf pan or glass pan.
Preheat oven to 400 degrees.
Spray loaf pan or rub with oil.

Put small amount of olive oil in a skillet over medium heat; cook and stir bell pepper, carrots, and onion until softened, 5 to 10 minutes. Add garlic for 1 to 2 minutes.

Mix with your hands the ground beef, bread crumbs, egg, skillet vegetables, salt, pepper, and milk into a large bowl. Press meat mixture into loaf pan. Bake 35 to 40 minutes.

Spread sauce on the top and bake 5 minutes more.

Healthy Herb-Rubbed Roasted Pork Tenderloin with Onions and Broccoli

SERVES: 4-5 | CALORIES: 350 (for 2 – 3 slices roasted pork and vegetables)

Ingredients

- 1½ to 2 pound pork tenderloin (or 4 pork loin chops)
- seasoned salt (without MSG)
- Italian seasoning (optional)
- 2 medium yellow or white onions, halved, sliced lengthwise into ¼ inch strips and pulled apart
- large broccoli heads, cut into bite sized pieces
- ¼ cup of olive oil
- full container of small grape tomatoes, halved (about 35 tomatoes)
- ¼ cup lemon juice
- salt and pepper, lemon pepper

Directions

Heat oven to 450 degrees. Rub pork with season salt and Italian seasoning.

Mix onion, broccoli, salt, pepper, additional Italian seasoning and ¼ cup olive oil.

Spread vegetables in a large glass/ceramic baking dish and lay pork on top.

Cook 25 - 30 minutes, flipping pork halfway through.

Remove pork and place on cutting board. Cover with foil.

Add halved tomatoes and lemon juice to vegetables. Roast 10 more minutes.

Slice pork into ¼ inch slices, or place individual pork chop on platter with vegetables and serve.

Add salt, pepper (or lemon pepper) as desired when serving.

Easy Slow Cooker Chicken Noodle Soup
SERVES: 10 | CALORIES: 160

Ingredients

- 1 tablespoon olive oil
- 2 yellow onions, chopped
- 1 large Idaho potato, cut into 1-inch cubes (leave skin on)
- 1 - 1½ pounds chicken breast
- 2 cups baby sliced carrots (approximately 2 - 3 large carrots)
- 2 stalks celery, chopped
- 2 teaspoons sea salt (or more to taste)
- 1 teaspoon black pepper
- 1 tablespoon Italian seasoning (or oregano)
- two 32-ounce cartons low-sodium organic chicken stock
- dry/uncooked egg noodles - you will need 8 - 12 ounces
- optional – fresh parsley, roughly chopped

Directions

Pour the olive oil in a 6 - 7 quart slow cooker.

Add the chicken breasts, chicken stock, onions, carrots, potato, celery, salt, pepper, Italian seasoning, and cook on low for 6 - 8 hours.

Remove chicken. Shred or cut into medium-sized pieces.

Add 8 ounces (approximately 1/2 bag) of dried egg noodles and fresh parsley 30 minutes before you're ready to eat. Cover, and cook until noodles are soft.

Season with additional salt and pepper, if needed.

Serve and enjoy.

Healthy Baked Tilapia, Cod or Catfish

SERVES: 4 | CALORIES: 200

Ingredients

- 4 tilapia fillets (6 – 8 ounces each)
- 3 tablespoons olive oil
- 1 pat of butter, melted
- 3 tablespoons lemon juice
- 1½ teaspoons garlic powder
- seasoned salt (without MSG)
- 2 tablespoons capers, drained (optional, but recommended)
- ½ teaspoon dried oregano (or Italian seasoning)

Directions

Place tilapia in an ungreased 13 x 9 inch baking dish. In a small bowl, combine the oil, butter, lemon juice, garlic powder and seasoned salt; pour over the fillets.

Top with capers and oregano (or Italian seasoning.)

Bake, uncovered, at 425 degrees until fish just begins to flake easily with a fork, 10 - 15 minutes (may take 20 minutes if Cod or Catfish.)

(Serve green beans, broccoli, and/or a salad with meal.)

One Pot Skillet Lasagna: A Thirty Minute Meal!

SERVES: 4-5 | CALORIES: 450 (one serving is 1/5 of the total recipe)

Ingredients

- 1 pound ground turkey or ground chicken
- 1 bell pepper chopped into small pieces
- ½ onion, diced
- 1 large carrot, shredded
- 1 small zucchini, shredded
- 1 ½ teaspoons salt, ¼ teaspoon pepper
- 1 teaspoon minced garlic, 1 teaspoon Italian seasoning
- ½ teaspoon dried oregano / 1 pinch red pepper flakes
- 14 ounce can petite (or diced) tomatoes with garlic and basil
- 3 cups low sodium chicken broth
- dry/uncooked lasagna noodles (about 9 regular noodles)
- 1 cup shredded mozzarella cheese

Directions

Cook ground turkey in a large pot over medium heat for 2-3 minutes or until starting to brown.

Add bell pepper and onion to the pot and cook for about 5 additional minutes, stirring occasionally, until turkey is browned and veggies are almost tender.

Add carrot, zucchini, salt, pepper, garlic, Italian seasoning, oregano and a pinch of pepper flakes to the pot. Stir and cook for 1 minute.

Add tomatoes, chicken broth and 9 broken lasagna noodles to the pot - stir well. Bring to a simmer over medium-high heat (approximately 2 minutes).

Reduce heat to medium. Cover the pot but stir often until lasagna noodles are just tender (or to desired tenderness) — about 10 to 15 minutes maximum.

Sprinkle with 1 cup mozzarella cheese, cover again and let sit for 5 minutes.

Serve immediately.

Healthy Chicken Fajitas
SERVES: 4 | CALORIES: 200 per filled tortilla

Ingredients

- 4 skinless chicken breasts (sliced into ¼ inch strips)
- 2 red, green or yellow bell peppers (cut lengthwise into ½ inch strips)
- 2 small red onions, halved and sliced thin (pull slices apart by hand)
- 12 soft flour tortillas (not hard taco shells)
- olive or vegetable oil / salt and pepper
- 2 teaspoons of chili powder
- ¼ cup of lime juice (or lemon juice)
- 2 tablespoons of cilantro (Use dry oregano if cilantro is unavailable)
- 2 tablespoons of Worcestershire sauce
- 1 teaspoon of brown sugar
- (optional toppings) salsa, hot sauce, sour cream

Directions

Heat a tablespoon of oil in a nonstick skillet over medium-high heat. Place chicken in skillet and cook 6 to 8 minutes on first side. Flip and repeat on second side.

Place the cooked chicken strips into a large bowl that contains the mixture of lime juice, cilantro, Worcestershire, sugar, salt and 2 tablespoons of oil.

To the skillet, add bell peppers, onions, chili powder, salt, pepper and ¼ cup (splash) of water to pan. Cook over medium heat for 5 - 6 minutes.

Add the chicken back into the skillet to warm for 1 more minute.
Transfer the contents of the skillet to a platter or bowl or serve from the skillet.

Warm the tortillas as directed on the package, or place one in the microwave for 15 seconds when needed.

Add chicken and vegetables to a tortilla.

Top with salsa, hot sauce and sour cream (optional) as desired. Enjoy!

Simple, Delicious Roasted Vegetables
(Low Calorie and Highly Nutritious!)
CALORIES: 30 to 40 per serving (approximately)

Ingredients

- broccoli (cut into florets)
- green beans
- asparagus (cut an inch off the stalks bottom)
- cauliflower (cut into florets) - note below for Buffalo cauliflower
- butternut squash (cubed)
- Brussels sprouts (cut in halves)
- carrots (cut into ½ inch pieces) - mixing with other vegetables works well
- olive oil, Italian spices, salt, pepper, lemon juice, yellow onion

Directions

Heat oven to 350 degrees.

Place your selected vegetable pieces into a bowl. One exception - asparagus should be laid on the baking tray and rolled in the mixture below.

Add 2 or 3 tablespoons olive oil, sprinkle in Italian spices (or oregano), salt and pepper and mix by hand to coat the vegetables (add 2 tablespoons of lemon juice for extra zest).

Place vegetables on baking tray and cook for 30 minutes.

NOTE: Add a large sweet yellow onion to any dish above – cut onion in half lengthwise. Cut into ¼ or ½ inch slices and pull apart by hand so you have long strips. Mix with your vegetable selection. The onion slices will become a crowd favorite.

Some Extra Taste Pleasers

Butternut squash and Brussels sprouts: get some reduced balsamic vinegar (fig, black cherry, or any flavor) and squirt a thin strip onto the sprouts before serving.

Cauliflower: Add a small amount of Buffalo wing sauce to your bowl and mix with the other ingredients to coat the florets. It is guaranteed to please any palate that likes spicy chicken wings. Adds aproximately 10 calories per serving.

Garlic: Add chopped garlic (2 or 3 cloves) to the mixture of any vegetable to add a delicate, nutty flavor.

40

Audretta Hall has spent over 15 years speaking at events, on podcasts and on radio shows about the health benefits of listening to your body. In addition to losing close to 100 pounds herself, Audretta has helped hundreds of other people lose thousands of pounds via easy-to-follow adjustments in their daily routines and eating habits.

Audretta often says, "I believe that we truly live in a miracle. Just give your body what it needs and it will reset itself."

She gained her life-changing information through certification as a nutritional counselor, and throughout her own personal health journey. Audretta happily counsels thousands of people each day by way of her health and wellness posts.

Robert Krumroy is a nationally recognized speaker and author of 11 books. This is the fifth in a series of books for elementary school children that encourages character building, kindness, motivation, personal responsibility, thinking big, evolving future dreams, and understanding what foods are most healthy.

The book is sponsored by the Bikes for Kids Foundation and is being used in schools from North Carolina to California. Robert lives in Greensboro, NC.

Ugur Kose grew up in Amasya, one of the smallest villages in Turkey. He loved comics as a little boy and created his first comic book character when he was 12. Ugur studied mechanical engineering in high school and aeronautical engineering at university. After graduating with a degree in engineering he worked in that field for a few years, but eventually returned to what he calls "the magical world of illustration." Ugur has now delighted in illustrating children's books for over 20 years, contributing to over 1,000 books in that period! He is proud to work each day in his personal studio, bringing stories to life and making his own dreams come true.

Donna West has worked as a creative director and designer of books, videos, event marketing, print, radio and TV advertising for over two decades. She has won praise for designing financial industry classics, as well as 12 Addy Awards for her work with Fortune 50 organizations and small businesses.

Donna's dream - to not only design children's books but also to help with an amazing children's charity - comes true daily via Kids Dreams Matter Publishing and Bikes For Kids Foundation. Donna lives in Kernersville, NC.